D1061965

Kids Have Rights Too!

Library of Congress Cataloging-in-Publication Data

Scott, Janine.
Kids have rights too! / by Janine Scott.
p. cm. -- (Shockwave)
Includes index.
ISBN-10: 0-531-17763-7 (lib. bdg.)
ISBN-13: 978-0-531-17763-1 (lib. bdg.)
ISBN-10: 0-531-18838-8 (pbk.)
ISBN-13: 978-0-531-18838-5 (pbk.)
1. Children's rights--Juvenile literature. 2. Child labor--Juvenile literature. I. Title. II. Series.

HQ789.S36 2008
323.3'52--dc22

2007019446

Published in 2008 by Children's Press, an imprint of Scholastic Inc.,
557 Broadway, New York, New York 10012
www.scholastic.com

08 09 10 11 12 13 14 15 16 17
10 9 8 7 6 5 4 3 2 1

Printed in China through Colorcraft Ltd., Hong Kong

Author: Janine Scott
Educational Consultant: Ian Morrison
Editor: Janine Scott
Designer: Emma Alsweiler
Photo Researcher: Janine Scott

Photographs by: Big Stock Photo (p. 34); **Courtesy of Big Brothers Big Sisters/www.bbbs.org** (p. 31); © **Courtesy of Free The Children/www.freethechildren.com** (p. 29); **Courtesy of RugMark Foundation/www.rugmark.org** (class, pp. 30–31); **Courtesy of Street Kids International/www.streetkids.org** (p. 30); **Getty Images** (cover; pp. 14–15; p. 22; boy in wheelchair, p. 23; p. 24; p. 26); **Photodisc** (pp. 8–9); **Photolibrary** (girl weaving, p. 25; chimney sweeps, p. 11; UNICEF outreach, p. 21); **Stock Central/Topfoto** (p. 10); **Tranz/Corbis** (p. 3; p. 7; girl in textiles factory, pp. 10–11; pp. 12–13; pp. 16–20; child soldier, p. 21; sewing class, p. 23; newspaper delivery boy, p. 25; p. 28; child workers, pp. 32–33)

SHOCKWAVE
SOCIAL STUDIES

Kids Have Rights Too!

Janine Scott

children's press®
An imprint of Scholastic Inc.
NEW YORK • TORONTO • LONDON • AUCKLAND • SYDNEY
MEXICO CITY • NEW DELHI • HONG KONG
DANBURY, CONNECTICUT

CHECK THESE OUT!

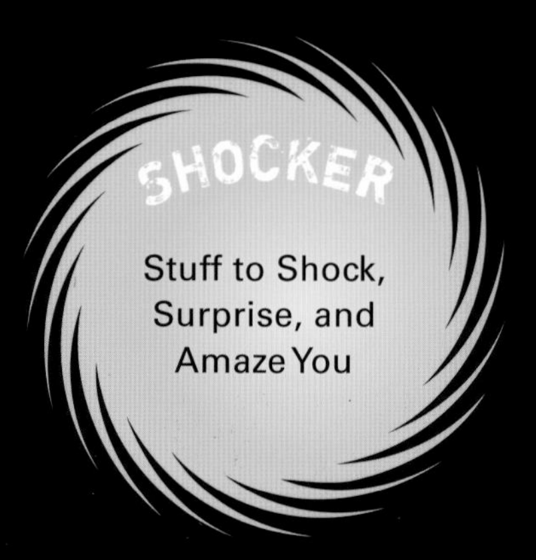

Quick Recaps and Notable Notes

Word Stunners and Other Oddities

The Heads-Up on Expert Reading

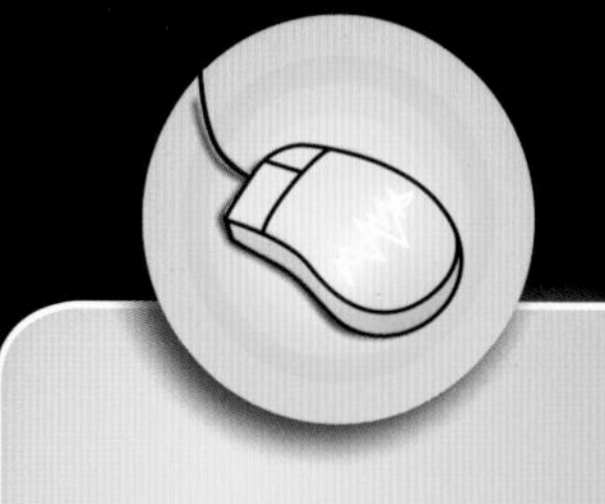

Links to More Information

CONTENTS

HIGH-POWERED WORDS

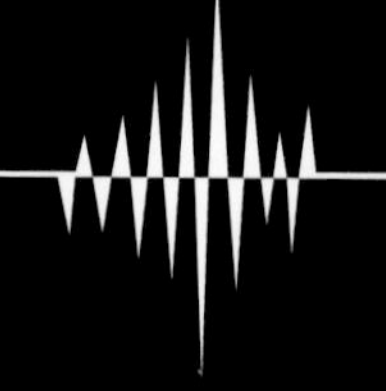

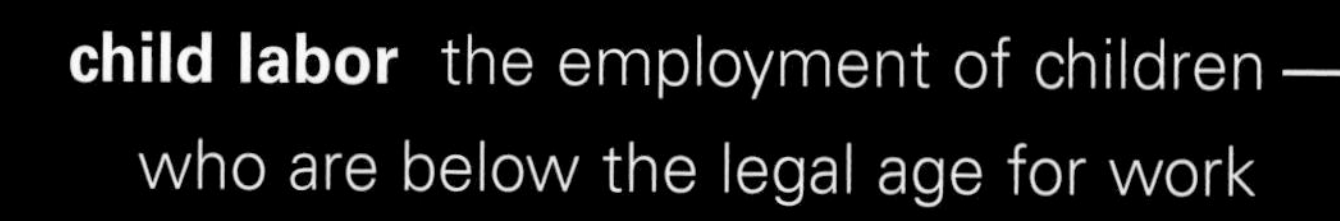

child labor the employment of children who are below the legal age for work

exploitation (*eks ploi TAY shuhn*) taking unfair advantage of someone or something

manufacturing large-scale production using machines

rights the freedom, equal treatment, and resources that are guaranteed by law

strike an organized work stoppage arising from a disagreement between workers and their employer

sweatshop a factory or workshop that has harsh and unsafe working conditions

United Nations an international organization of countries that promotes world peace and human dignity

For additional vocabulary, see Glossary on page 34.

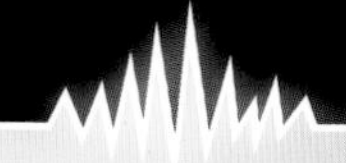

It is not certain where the term *strike* came from. However, it is thought that it is related to the eighteenth-century term *striking* – a term for lowering a ship's sail, indicating a refusal to sail.

Today, many children around the world have been granted **rights** by law. Today, we believe that children have the right to an education and health care. They have the right to be protected from harm, the right to their opinions, and the right to play. Play helps young children explore their world and develop social skills. It allows them to have a childhood. However, the modern notion of childhood came about only in the last hundred or so years. In the past, farming was a way of survival for most families. Many children were put to work at an early age. They worked alongside their parents planting crops, caring for animals, or plowing fields. There was little time for schooling or sports or leisure activities.

Child or Adult?

Have you heard the saying "stop being a child"? The legal age at which a child becomes an adult is different in different countries. It can even vary within the same country. For example, in some parts of the United States, children can leave school at sixteen but cannot vote until they are eighteen. The age at which a child becomes an adult is called the "age of majority." That is why children are called "minors."

	U.S.A.	Australia	Britain	Japan	India
Leave school	16–18	15	16	15	14
Marry	18	18	18	20	18 (girl), 21 (boy)
Vote	18	18	18	20	18
Drive a car	14–16	16	17	18	18
Adult	18–21	18	18	20	18

Child Workers

In the past, most children worked, so they didn't go to school. In the 1700s, most of the world's population lived in rural places and worked in agriculture. Children worked for their families. Families had to farm to earn a living and feed themselves. Farmwork had its quieter times during the shorter winter days. Families usually cared for their children's well-being.

Then, in about 1760, the **Industrial Revolution** began in Britain. It spread to the United States in the early 1800s. Many people left the countryside to work in the cities. Machines and **manufacturing** became a big part of working life. Children swapped their jobs in the fields for work in factories and mines. With their small bodies, they were employed to duck under fast-moving machines in factories, or to haul coal along narrow passages deep under the ground. Children had few rights back then. The working conditions were harsh, and the punishment for speaking out was harsh too. The rights of children and the rights of workers were unheard of in the 1700s. Those rights were not to be considered until much later.

Paragraphs make reading easier. They separate different topics. When I come to a new paragraph, I always try to find the "topic sentence" (usually the first). This helps me anticipate the rest of the paragraph.

Woman pulling coal wagon while two children push

During the Industrial Revolution, there was a huge demand for coal, which powered factory machines and steam engines. Many workers were needed to extract the coal. Bosses often employed women and children because they could pay them less than men. Children as young as five were sent down into the coal mines. They often worked 18-hour days.

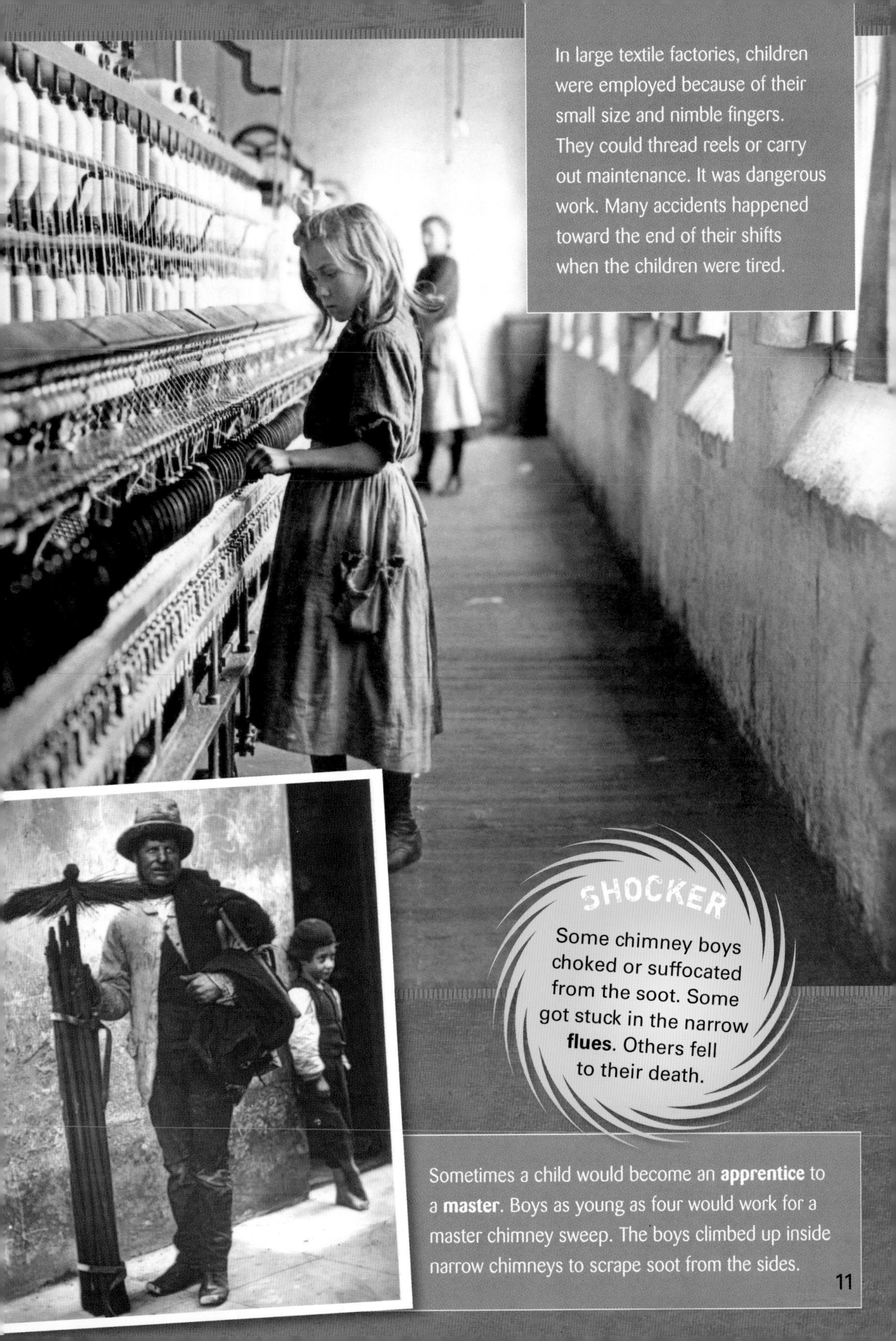

In large textile factories, children were employed because of their small size and nimble fingers. They could thread reels or carry out maintenance. It was dangerous work. Many accidents happened toward the end of their shifts when the children were tired.

SHOCKER

Some chimney boys choked or suffocated from the soot. Some got stuck in the narrow **flues**. Others fell to their death.

Sometimes a child would become an **apprentice** to a **master**. Boys as young as four would work for a master chimney sweep. The boys climbed up inside narrow chimneys to scrape soot from the sides.

Sweatshop Children

During the 1800s, millions of **immigrants** from Europe poured into America. They settled in cities such as New York and Detroit. They provided an instant workforce for the thousands of factories and **sweatshops** that existed. Sweatshops were workplaces where goods were manufactured by the "sweating" system. In this system, big factories hired people who would carry out the actual work in their smaller factories. These "factories" were often people's homes. In summer, sweatshops were just as the name suggests. There was often no ventilation, so temperatures were stifling. People sweated over their machines, working long hours for very little money. By 1910, there were about 30,000 sweatshops in New York City alone. In the United States, during the early 1900s, about two million children worked.

Many immigrant families lived in overcrowded **tenement** housing. They often converted their tiny apartments into sweatshops. Children as young as three used to help their family earn a living by sewing on buttons, making artificial flowers, or even rolling cigars. Sometimes children were employed to run errands or deliver bundles from one sweatshop to another. **Child labor** was widespread. Children were paid low wages, but, more importantly, they were less likely to complain about their working conditions.

This is the Basso family, who lived in New York City in 1912. They made artificial roses for a living. They lived in a one-room tenement apartment. In a 13-hour workday, the whole family could make as many as 3,168 roses. However, this was only enough to buy one meal for one person.

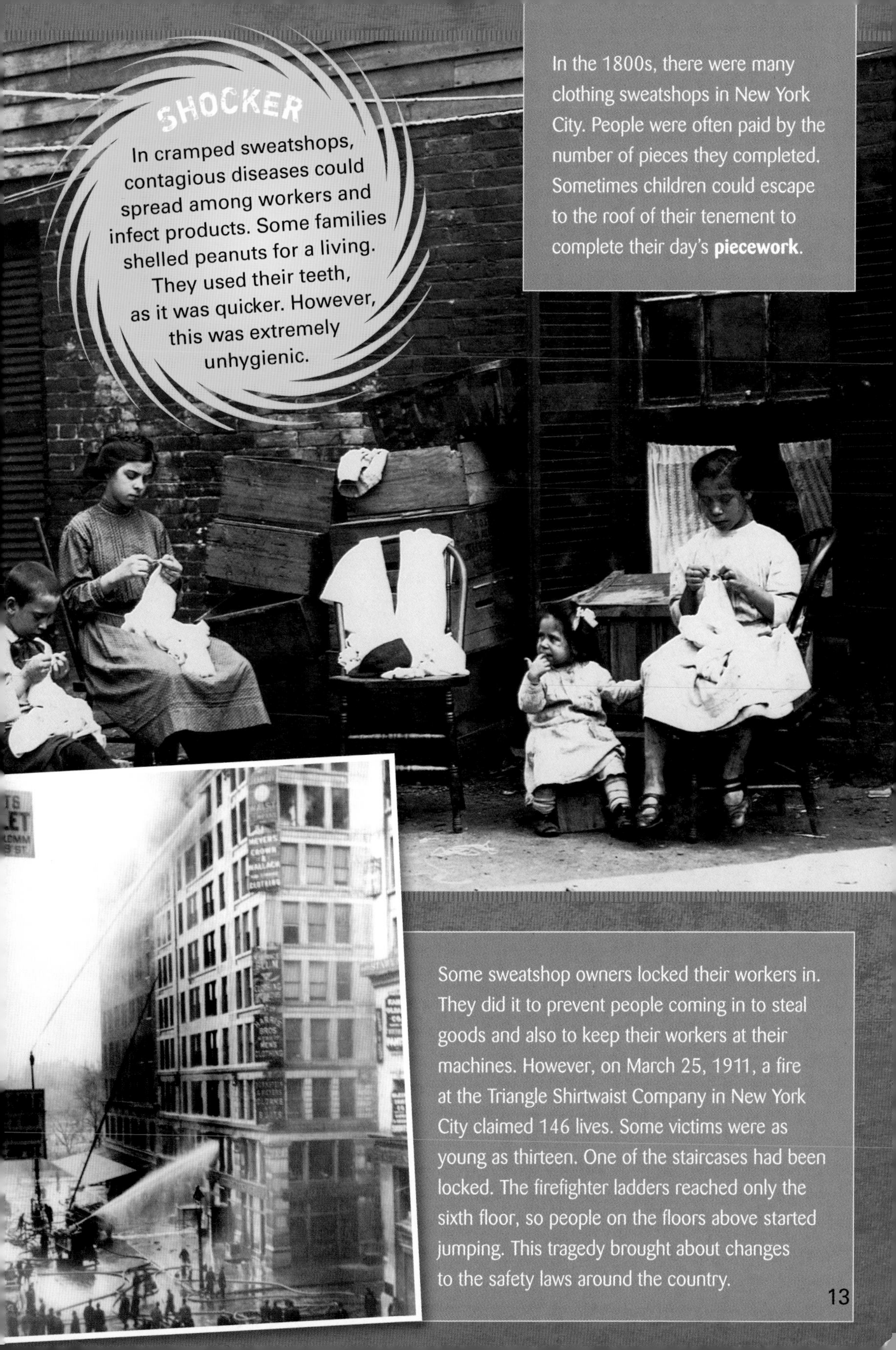

In the 1800s, there were many clothing sweatshops in New York City. People were often paid by the number of pieces they completed. Sometimes children could escape to the roof of their tenement to complete their day's **piecework**.

SHOCKER

In cramped sweatshops, contagious diseases could spread among workers and infect products. Some families shelled peanuts for a living. They used their teeth, as it was quicker. However, this was extremely unhygienic.

Some sweatshop owners locked their workers in. They did it to prevent people coming in to steal goods and also to keep their workers at their machines. However, on March 25, 1911, a fire at the Triangle Shirtwaist Company in New York City claimed 146 lives. Some victims were as young as thirteen. One of the staircases had been locked. The firefighter ladders reached only the sixth floor, so people on the floors above started jumping. This tragedy brought about changes to the safety laws around the country.

Protecting Children

In 1875, two Americans, Henry Bergh and Elbridge Gerry, came to the aid of child workers. They founded the Society for the Prevention of Cruelty to Children (SPCC). In 1884, the group tried to get child-labor **legislation** passed in New York state. The legislation proposed that children under twenty-one could work only a ten-hour day, six days a week, and that children under fourteen couldn't work in factories. But there was a great deal of opposition to the legislation. Factory owners threatened to move their businesses to other states that didn't have child-labor laws. Even the parents of the child workers disapproved. Many of the families relied on the money that their children brought in.

The group had some success though. In 1886, a law called the Factory Act was passed in New York State. Children under thirteen could no longer work in factories in rural areas. However, the law proved fairly ineffective. There was just one person inspecting all the factories in the entire state, and that person had to file a report only once a year!

Newspaper vendor, 1910

Many children sold new
the streets until midnigh
even froze to death duri
Girl newspaper vendors
common as boys. In so
girls had to be age sixte
newspapers, whereas b
young as ten. Often ch
long hours, so there w
for schooling.

In the past, employers didn't have to ensure that their workers were safe at work. This photo was taken in 1907 in Corinth, Kentucky. Fourteen-year-old Luther Watson lost his right arm in a saw accident at a box factory. He went on to attend school.

SHOCKER

The large machines in textile factories could cause serious injuries. Children could have an arm ripped off if loose clothing got caught. They could even be **scalped** if their hair got caught.

Firsts in Labor Laws

Britain, 1802

Britain passes the first child-labor law – children under nine who depend on charity cannot work in cotton mills. Children under fourteen can work for only 12 hours a day, and cannot work at night.

United States, 1836

Massachusetts passes the first state child-labor law – children under fifteen can work in factories only if they have attended school for three months the previous year.

Child-Labor Events 1700s–1886

1700s – mostly farmwork
1760 – Industrial Revolution
1800s – rise of sweatshops
1802 – 1st child-labor law in Britain
1836 – 1st state child-labor law in U.S.A.
1875 – SPCC founded
1886 – Factory Act passed

Documenting Children

In 1904, another social reform group was set up. The National Child Labor Committee's aim was to highlight the plight of child workers in the United States. In 1907, the group hired photographer Lewis Wickes Hine to document child labor. Hine captured children working in factories, mines, fields, and sweatshops. His compelling photographs helped to bring to public attention the problem of child labor. For the next eleven years, he traveled the United States taking photographs. He was unwelcome in many workplaces. Sometimes, in order to get into a factory, he would disguise himself as a fire inspector.

Hine not only took photographs. He also took notes about many of the children he met, such as their name, age, and how long they had worked. However, many employers, parents, and even the children themselves lied about their age. To judge how old children were, Hine noted their height using the buttons on his vest. Hine also wrote essays and had them published in magazines and newspapers. He gave lectures and slide shows.

I wasn't sure what "documenting" meant. But after finishing the first paragraph, it was clear that it meant "gathering and reporting on evidence." Many new words can be figured out by simply continuing to read.

In 1913, Hine photographed these children working in a cotton field in Bells, Texas. It was hot, backbreaking work. Most of the cotton was picked by children under fourteen years of age.

In Britain in the 1800s, one factory boss thought that a boy was working too slowly. His nailed the boy's ear to a table for punishment!

Breaker boys worked in coal mines. They sat bent over coal chutes or fast-moving belts for 12 hours a day. Their job was to pick out slate and other stone that could not burn that was mixed up with the coal. It was dangerous work. The children could fall onto the belts, or get fragments of coal in their eyes. When children started out on the job, their skin was not tough, so their hands would swell and crack open.

Work Hazards

Glass factory	High temperatures and toxic fumes harmed eyes and caused lung diseases.
Sugar-beet field	Children cut their legs when they topped beets with large, sharp knives. They carried as much as 40 pounds of beets, resulting in back pain.
Shrimp cannery	The shrimp released a chemical that ate into the children's hands, making their hands bleed and skin peel.

The girl in this canning factory had to sit on two wooden boxes in order to reach the workbench.

Striking for Rights

Child workers had few rights. However, that didn't mean that some of them didn't stand up for their rights. Some banded together and went on **strike** to fight for better wages and fewer working hours. They demanded safer working conditions. Sometimes strikes led to big changes. Sometimes the strikers made no difference.

On June 1, 1903, 16,000 children from 600 mills in Pennsylvania didn't turn up for work. Hearing about the strike, 73-year-old Mary Harris Jones, or Mother Jones, got involved. She was a strong, determined figure in the U.S. labor movement. On June 17, Mother Jones and 6,000 children marched to the city hall in Kensington, Pennsylvania. Feeling that their demonstration had not been effective, Mother Jones planned another one. On July 7, she led 300 women, men, and children on a 125-mile march to Long Island, where President Theodore Roosevelt was vacationing. After walking for 22 days, they were refused a meeting with the president. However, they succeeded in bringing the children's plight to the nation's attention.

Mother Jones

Child Strikers!

Date: July 1828, Paterson, New Jersey
Strikers: Cotton-mill workers
Wanted: Lunch hour changed from 1:00 to original time of 12 noon; 13.5-hour day changed to 10-hour day
Duration of strike: three weeks
Result: Original lunch hour restored; no reduction in hours; strike leaders fired

Date: July 20, 1899, New York City
Strikers: Newspaper vendors, or newsies
Wanted: To buy 100 newspapers for 50 cents instead of 60 cents (they sold them for 1 cent); wanted to return unsold papers
Duration of strike: two weeks
Result: Price stayed the same, but could refund unsold papers

WE Want to Go to School

More School Less Hospital

WE ARE protected by a tariff.

Reasons to Strike

- low wages
- long working hours
- harsh working conditions
- no time to attend school

These child mill workers from Kensington, Pennsylvania, wanted to work for only 55 hours per week, rather than 60. When the mill owners refused, the children went on strike on June 1, 1903.

SHOCKER

One company boss got a real shock in July 1899 when **messengers** went on strike. His own son was one of the strikers!

Newspaper boys hung around theaters and stores to sell their papers. They also jumped onto moving streetcars to sell to the passengers. This was very dangerous and sometimes resulted in the child's loss of an arm or a leg. However, a missing limb could be good for business. People would often buy from a **maimed** child.

Children's Rights

The rights that most children have today were part of the outcome of World Wars I and II. In 1919, a year after the end of World War I, a British woman named Eglantyne Jebb founded the Save the Children Fund to help hungry German and Austrian children who had been affected by the war. Then, in 1923, Jebb wrote a set of children's rights. She believed children should be treated with respect. A year later, the **League of Nations** adopted Jebb's list. It became known as the Declaration of the Rights of the Child.

On October 24, 1945, a month after the end of World War II, the **United Nations** (UN) was established. The aim of this organization of nations was to promote world peace and human rights. In 1946, the UN established the United Nations Children's Fund (UNICEF). Its purpose was to provide food, clothing, and medicine to children who were victims of the war.

In 1948, the UN adopted an important document concerning human rights. During the war, many Europeans had lost most or all of their human rights. However, children had to wait until 1989 to get their own UN document, the Convention on the Rights of the Child. The document was designed to help protect the rights of children and prevent child labor. Jebb's list of children's rights from 1923 formed the basis of this document.

In 1948, UNICEF provided care for European children affected by World War II. Here children in Vienna, Austria, receive free food and drink.

Political unrest and war can lead to children's loss of their families, homes, rights, and even lives. Many children also become child soldiers. There are more than 300,000 child soldiers around the world.

The Three P's

Almost every country in the world has signed the United Nations Convention on the Rights of the Child. It is based on three P's:

- Participation: meaning a child should participate in decisions affecting his or her life now and in the future
- Protection: meaning that a child should be kept safe from harmful acts, such as **exploitation**, warfare, and abuse
- Provision: meaning a child should have access to food, housing, health care, schooling, rest, and play

However, there are two other P words that often get in the way of all countries achieving the three P's for children. They are politics and poverty.

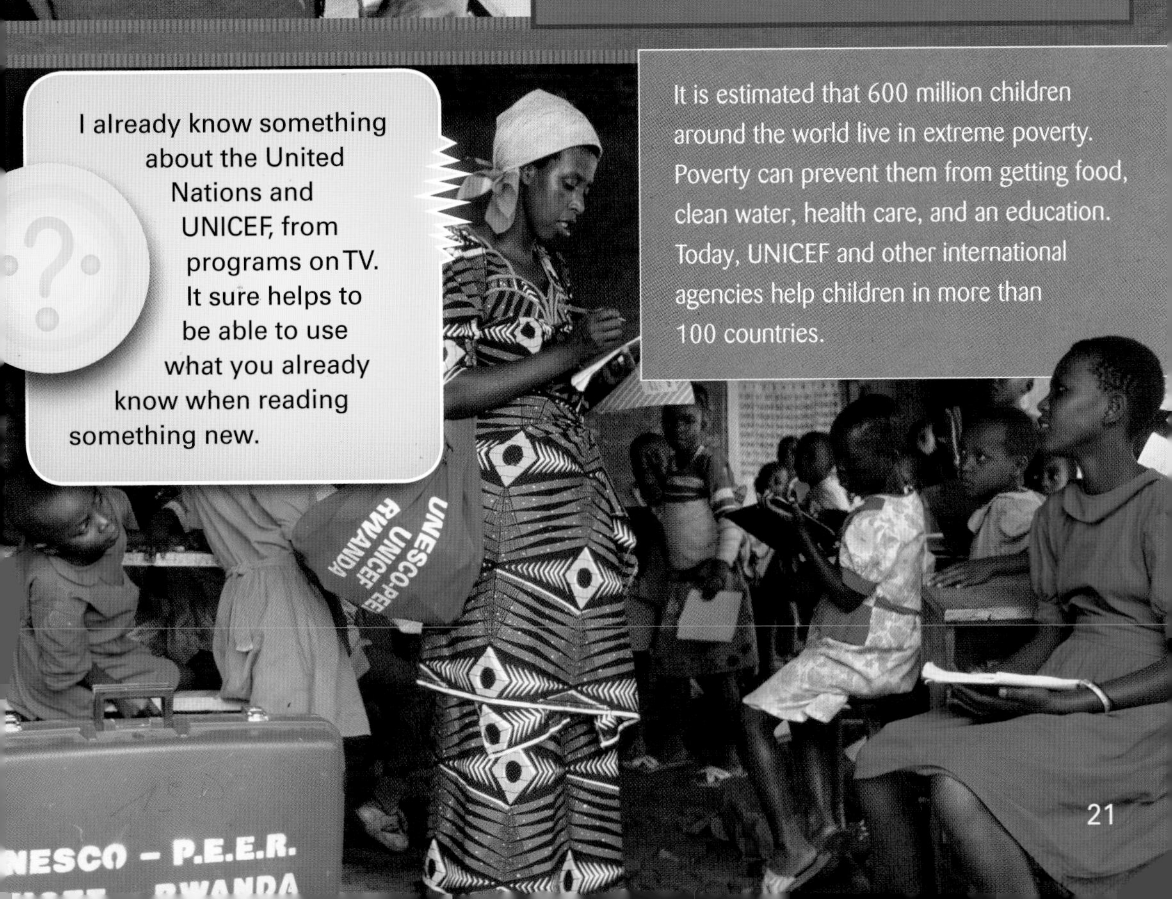

I already know something about the United Nations and UNICEF, from programs on TV. It sure helps to be able to use what you already know when reading something new.

It is estimated that 600 million children around the world live in extreme poverty. Poverty can prevent them from getting food, clean water, health care, and an education. Today, UNICEF and other international agencies help children in more than 100 countries.

The Right to Be Different

Children have a right to be different. Many children have a physical or mental **disability** that makes life very challenging. They deserve care and respect from others. In the past, people with disabilities were treated differently and often very badly. Fortunately, in the last few decades, laws have been passed to protect people with disabilities.

In the United States, the Americans with Disabilities Act (ADA) clamped down on **discrimination** based on disability. The act paved the way for physical changes to public places, such as creating wheelchair ramps in restaurants and libraries. It stated that guide dogs must now be allowed into public buildings. The act also regulates public transportation, civil rights, and employment opportunities for people with disabilities.

The Individuals with Disabilities Education Improvement Act (IDEA) states that children with disabilities should have the right to free, appropriate public education. Each child has an individualized education program (IEP). It is designed to help the child reach his or her full learning potential.

Different Rights for Different Abilities?

Children with learning disabilities are eligible for special accommodations. Should gifted children, who may have different learning styles too, have the right to special services? Some schools voluntarily provide specialized education for gifted children. Others have cut the program from their budgets. However, if a gifted child has a disability, such as ADHD (Attention Deficit Hyperactivity Disorder), then the student will qualify for special education services. Do you think only children with disabilities have the right to a special education?

Children with disabilities have the right to take part in regular school programs. This is called mainstreaming. Some schools run classes that cater to the special needs of disabled children. This allows the children not only to benefit from teachers who are specially trained to help disabled children, but also to socialize with nondisabled children.

The *dis-* prefix is often attached to a word to express its opposite, as in *ability/disability*. Other *dis-* words are *dislike*, *disobedient*, and *disloyal*. Other prefixes that form opposites include *un-*, *in-*, *im-*, *non-*, *il-*, and *ir-*.

One of the educational aims for children with intellectual disabilities is to give them life skills so that they can become independent adults. These young people in China attend a special school for children with intellectual disabilities. They are having a sewing lesson.

Work or Labor?

Every day, millions of children around the world go to work. Some children deliver newspapers. Others work in a family store or a fast-food restaurant. So what's the difference between youth employment and child labor? Youth employment is work exchanged for a wage, but so is child labor. The big difference is that child labor often takes unfair advantage of children. A child laborer may work long hours for low wages, or in conditions that put his or her health at risk. This definitely happened during the Industrial Revolution, and the problem hasn't gone away. There are millions of child laborers around the world.

On the other hand, youth employment can have many benefits. It can teach children valuable life skills and responsibilities, such as setting and achieving work-related goals, working as a group, and managing money and time. It also helps children develop independence. However, some people argue that even a part-time job can interfere with a child's progress at school. They say that the child is too tired to learn at school, or doesn't have enough time to complete homework. This, they argue, could in turn limit the kinds of jobs available to the child as an adult.

Some children work hard every day, but they are not being exploited. They are simply carrying out their daily chores. In many countries, children collect firewood for the day's cooking or carry drinking water from a well. They often walk for miles.

Many children hold part-time jobs before and after school. The minimum age for most employment is fourteen. However, there are some exceptions to the child-labor laws. Children who are eleven years or older can deliver newspapers.

U.S. Federal Child-Labor Laws

Time and hour prohibitions for work by children aged fourteen and fifteen:

- not during school hours
- not before 7:00 A.M. or after 7:00 P.M. (9:00 P.M. from June 1 through Labor Day)
- not more than three hours on a school day (including Fridays)
- not more than eight hours a day on any nonschool day
- not more than 40 hours a week (Sunday through Saturday) in nonschool weeks

Youth Employment

Pro	Con
• manage money and time	• interferes with school
• set and achieve goals	• makes children tired
• develop independence	• takes time away from more important things

Egypt is known for its traditional handmade carpets. Some Egyptian children are carpet weavers. Today, many carpet factories run schools so that the children can receive an education. The training is sponsored by the Ministry of Education and Egypt's carpet industry. The children learn the art of weaving in the morning. In the afternoon, they attend regular school lessons.

Few Rights

In the past, children who were slaves often used to perform the same jobs as the children who were free. However, slave children were the master's property, so they didn't get paid. Free children could leave their job if they were unhappy, but slave children didn't have such freedom.

There are still children around the world who are like slave workers. They are called **bonded laborers**. Sometimes extremely poor families exchange the labor of a child or even the whole family for money. They are forced to work until the debt is paid off. However, the debt, although often very small, can take years to repay. It can even be handed down to the next generation.

In some countries, girls have fewer rights than boys. Boys and girls often have different responsibilities within their families. Girls might be expected to clean, cook, and take care of younger siblings. Because of this, many girls may be denied opportunities, such as getting an education, that many people consider to be rights.

SHOCKER

There are about 250 million child laborers around the world.

Many young children do physically challenging work. These girls in India are breaking rocks at a mine. Strenuous physical work can lead to long-term damage, because a child's body is still developing.

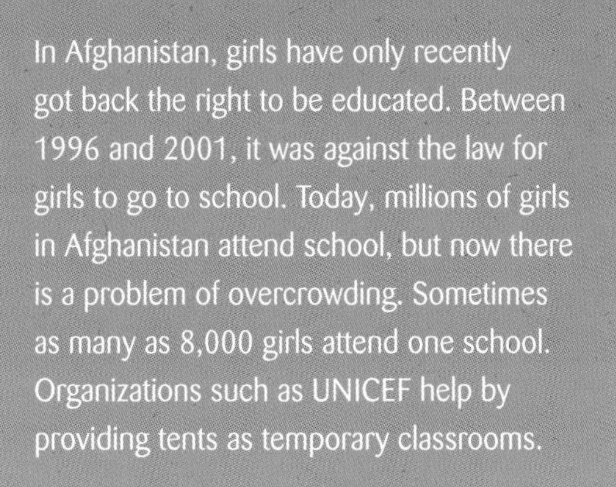

In Afghanistan, girls have only recently got back the right to be educated. Between 1996 and 2001, it was against the law for girls to go to school. Today, millions of girls in Afghanistan attend school, but now there is a problem of overcrowding. Sometimes as many as 8,000 girls attend one school. Organizations such as UNICEF help by providing tents as temporary classrooms.

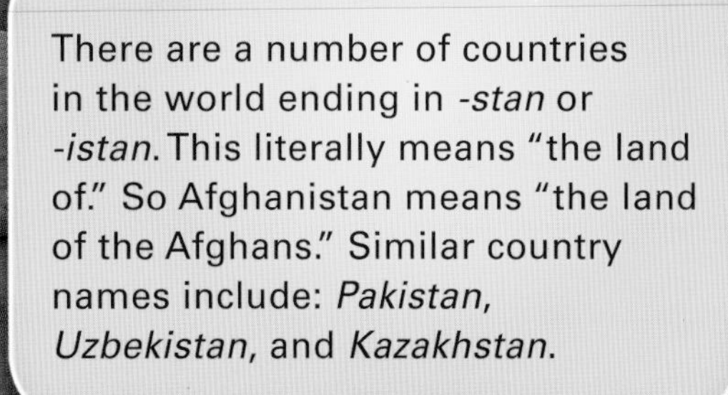

There are a number of countries in the world ending in *-stan* or *-istan*. This literally means "the land of." So Afghanistan means "the land of the Afghans." Similar country names include: *Pakistan*, *Uzbekistan*, and *Kazakhstan*.

Homelessness is a problem for millions of children all over the world. Sometimes a government or charitable organization provides shelters, such as these tents supplied to the homeless of Paris. But often, children live on the streets on their own, without parents, family, or shelter. Sometimes this is because family members have died or have become separated by war, or because families cannot afford to support their children. Sometimes children have run away from people who were exploiting them as child laborers.

Two Kids, Two Worlds

Kids can make a difference and bring about change. Here are two children who came from very different worlds, but shared the same goal – to stop bonded child labor.

Iqbal Masih was born in Pakistan in 1983. His parents sold him for twelve dollars to an owner of a carpet factory. Iqbal was only four years old at the time. The factory owner would chain Iqbal to a carpet loom and make him work 13 hours a day, six days a week. However, one day, when he was ten, Iqbal went to a Freedom Day rally. A human rights organization called the Bonded Labor Liberation Front (BLLF) was holding the rally. It opposed forced labor. Iqbal was so inspired that he never returned to the factory. He become an activist for BLLF and helped free thousands of children from bonded labor. Iqbal went on to attend school and planned to become a lawyer. In 1994, he won a Human Rights Youth in Action Award. Sadly, a year later, Iqbal began receiving death threats. A few weeks later, at the age of twelve, he was murdered.

Iqbal and other child laborers from Pakistan protested against child labor. Their banners read: "Don't buy children's blood."

More than one million children in 45 countries are involved in the organization Free the Children. Started by children for children, the organization is a good example of how young people can stand up for rights and change the world. These volunteers took some time out from building a school in India to have some fun in the mud. The organization thinks it is important that young volunteers learn how to work and play as a team.

Canadian Craig Kielburger is another child who has made a difference. In 1995, when he was twelve years old, he was touched by Iqbal's story and saddened by his death. He and 11 friends started an organization called Free the Children. Like Iqbal, they wanted to free children from bonded labor. That same year, Craig visited factories in India and Pakistan, where bonded child laborers work. Today, Free the Children is a worldwide organization. It has built more than 450 schools, set up health-care centers, and provided people with access to better sanitation and clean water.

Helping Kids

There are many organizations around the world whose aim is to stop child labor and the exploitation of children, to improve the lives of children, and to help children reach their potential.

Street Kids International raises awareness about the needs and rights of street kids around the world. The organization has worked with more than two million street kids in 60 countries. Youth workers hold workshops on work and education opportunities and health issues. In Zambia, the organization helped George, a street kid whose parents had died. He attended business training, and with a small loan, he set up his own market stall. Using his profits, he then returned to school, running his stall outside school hours.

RugMark is an international nonprofit organization. Its aim is to end child labor in the handmade-carpet industry in countries such as India, Nepal, and Pakistan. In South Asia, RugMark helps to free child workers from carpet factories. It sets up schools to help educate them. Carpets that have the RugMark label have not been made by child labor. Part of the money from each carpet sale helps pay for the education of former child laborers.

Big Brothers Big Sisters is a youth mentoring organization. It is often based in schools. For one hour a week, the child meets his or her mentor on a one-to-one basis. They talk, and the Big Brother or Big Sister offers friendship and guidance. The aim is to help children feel good about themselves. The organization's motto is "little moments, big magic." Here a girl spends time with her Big Sister mentor.

Around the world, there are about 250 million child laborers. Many work full-time in appalling conditions. Some make carpets. Some break rocks into gravel or pick coffee crops. Others clean streets or sift through garbage to sell. Many of them work to earn extra money for their families. Some are street kids, who need to support themselves.

Child workers in match factory, India

WHAT DO YOU THINK?

Should the UN enforce its international agreement?

PRO

I think that if the countries have agreed to the UN's plan, then they need to uphold it. Otherwise, they shouldn't have signed the agreement. I think that the UN should step in to ensure that everyone works toward achieving the rights set out in the declaration.

The United Nations (UN) set up an international agreement on children's rights in 1989. By 2003, all but two members of the UN had accepted the agreement. However, despite the UN agreement, millions of children around the world do not have the rights that are set out in the agreement. Poverty, war, and even greed can prevent these rights from being upheld. The UN says the agreement is simply a guide, and that no one can be forced to comply.

CON

I think the countries that signed the agreement *must* want to work toward getting all the rights for children accepted in their countries. But change takes time. People should realize that lots of circumstances could prevent children from getting basic necessities, such as food, shelter, safety, and schooling.

GLOSSARY

apprentice (*uh PREN tiss*) a person who learns a trade by working with a skilled person

bonded laborer a person who is forced to work for no pay, often to pay off a debt

disability physical or intellectual impairment

discrimination prejudice or unjust behavior based on differences in age, race, gender, or disability

flue a duct in a chimney

immigrant a person who arrives in a country to live

Industrial Revolution the rapid economic growth that began in England in 1760. Many industries became based on manufacturing rather than farming.

League of Nations an international organization established in 1920 to maintain world peace

legislation a law

maimed injured so that part of the body is permanently damaged

master a person expertly skilled in a particular trade or craft

messenger a person who carries a message

piecework work paid for according to the amount produced

scalp to cut or tear off the skin covering the top of the head

tenement a crowded apartment building whose residents are often low-income families

Tenement

FIND OUT MORE

BOOKS

Bartoletti, Susan Campbell. *Kids on Strike!* Houghton Mifflin, 2003.

Freedman, Russell. *Kids at Work: Lewis Hine and the Crusade Against Child Labor*. Clarion Books, 1998.

Kielburger, Marc and Kielburger, Craig. *Take Action!: A Guide to Active Citizenship*. John Wiley & Sons, 2002.

Lewis, Barbara A., Espeland, Pamela and Pernu, Caryn. *The Kid's Guide to Social Action: How to Solve the Social Problems You Choose – and Turn Creative Thinking Into Positive Action*. Free Spirit Publishing, 1998.

Newman, Shirlee P. *Child Slavery in Modern Times*. Franklin Watts, 2000.

WEB SITES

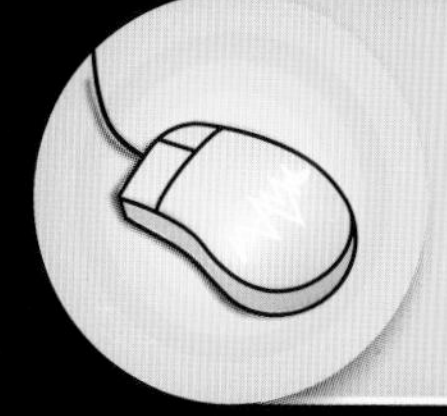

Go to the Web sites below to learn more about children's rights.

www.unicef.org/crcartoons

www.historyplace.com/unitedstates/childlabor/index.html

www.continuetolearn.uiowa.edu/laborctr/child_labor/about/us_history.html

http://library.thinkquest.org/5796/KIDS_RIGHTS.htm

INDEX

ABOUT THE AUTHOR

Janine Scott loves writing both fiction and nonfiction books for children. She really enjoyed writing this book. She is fascinated with history, and the Industrial Revolution certainly changed history. While Janine wrote this book at her comfortable desk in her comfortable office, she tried to imagine what it would have been like to duck under moving machinery to make repairs, or to squeeze down a chimney to clean off the soot. She tried to picture how she would have managed to work for 12 hours a day in a factory when she was just six years old. Janine greatly admires the courage of the working children who went on strike. She believes that children all around the world should have the right just to be kids.